HAL•LEONARD

GUITAR
PLAY•ALONG

Jack Johnson

VOL. 181

Photo courtesy of Brushfire Records

ISBN 978-1-4803-9514-5

cherry lane
music company

EXCLUSIVELY DISTRIBUTED BY
HAL•LEONARD®
CORPORATION
7777 W. BLUEMOUND RD. P.O. BOX 13819 MILWAUKEE, WI 53213

In Australia Contact:
Hal Leonard Australia Pty. Ltd.
4 Lentara Court
Cheltenham, Victoria, 3192 Australia
Email: ausadmin@halleonard.com.au

Visit Hal Leonard Online at
www.halleonard.com

Guitar Notation Legend

THE MUSICAL STAFF shows pitches and rhythms and is divided by bar lines into measures. Pitches are named after the first seven letters of the alphabet.

TABLATURE graphically represents the guitar fingerboard. Each horizontal line represents a string, and each number represents a fret.

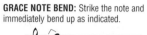

4th string, 2nd fret · 1st & 2nd strings open, played together · open D chord

HALF-STEP BEND: Strike the note and bend up 1/2 step.

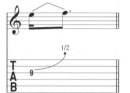

WHOLE-STEP BEND: Strike the note and bend up one step.

GRACE NOTE BEND: Strike the note and immediately bend up as indicated.

SLIGHT (MICROTONE) BEND: Strike the note and bend up 1/4 step.

BEND AND RELEASE: Strike the note and bend up as indicated, then release back to the original note. Only the first note is struck.

PRE-BEND: Bend the note as indicated, then strike it.

VIBRATO: The string is vibrated by rapidly bending and releasing the note with the fretting hand.

PALM MUTING: The note is partially muted by the pick hand lightly touching the string(s) just before the bridge.

HAMMER-ON: Strike the first (lower) note with one finger, then sound the higher note (on the same string) with another finger by fretting it without picking.

PULL-OFF: Place both fingers on the notes to be sounded. Strike the first note and without picking, pull the finger off to sound the second (lower) note.

LEGATO SLIDE: Strike the first note and then slide the same fret-hand finger up or down to the second note. The second note is not struck.

SHIFT SLIDE: Same as legato slide, except the second note is struck.

TRILL: Very rapidly alternate between the notes indicated by continuously hammering on and pulling off.

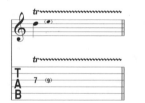

TAPPING: Hammer ("tap") the fret indicated with the pick-hand index or middle finger and pull off to the note fretted by the fret hand.

NATURAL HARMONIC: Strike the note while the fret-hand lightly touches the string directly over the fret indicated.

PINCH HARMONIC: The note is fretted normally and a harmonic is produced by adding the edge of the thumb or the tip of the index finger of the pick hand to the normal pick attack.

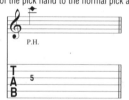

TREMOLO PICKING: The note is picked as rapidly and continuously as possible.

VIBRATO BAR DIVE AND RETURN: The pitch of the note or chord is dropped a specified number of steps (in rhythm), then returned to the original pitch.

VIBRATO BAR SCOOP: Depress the bar just before striking the note, then quickly release the bar.

VIBRATO BAR DIP: Strike the note and then immediately drop a specified number of steps, then release back to the original pitch.

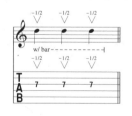

Additional Musical Definitions

 (accent) · Accentuate note (play it louder).

 (staccato) · Play the note short.

D.S. al Coda · Go back to the sign (𝄋), then play until the measure marked "***To Coda***," then skip to the section labelled "**Coda**."

D.C. al Fine · Go back to the beginning of the song and play until the measure marked "***Fine***" (end).

Fill · Label used to identify a brief melodic figure which is to be inserted into the arrangement.

N.C. · Harmony is implied.

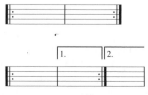 · Repeat measures between signs.

· When a repeated section has different endings, play the first ending only the first time and the second ending only the second time.

CONTENTS

Better Together

Words and Music by Jack Johnson

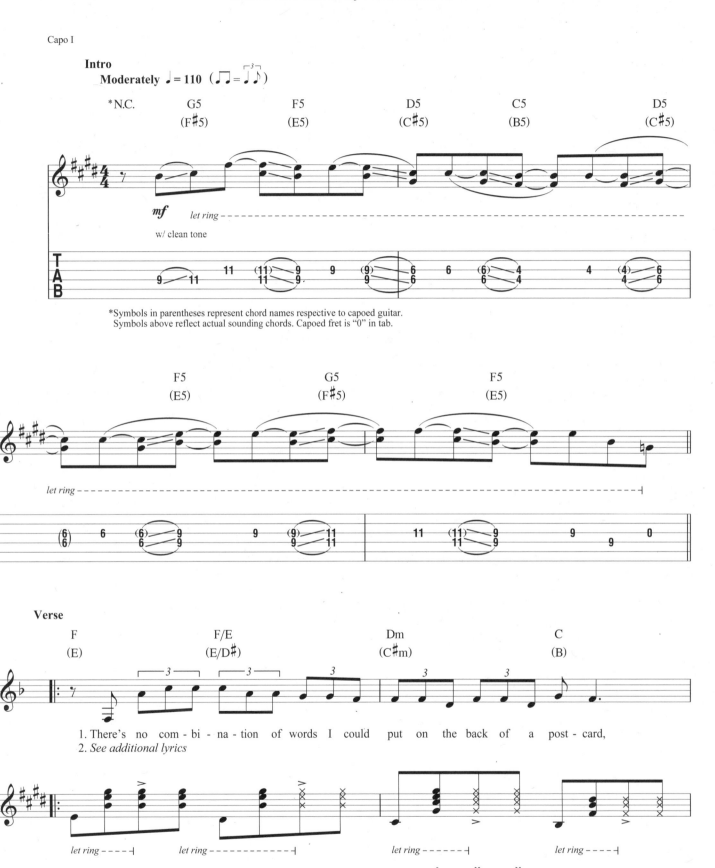

*Symbols in parentheses represent chord names respective to capoed guitar.
Symbols above reflect actual sounding chords. Capoed fret is "0" in tab.

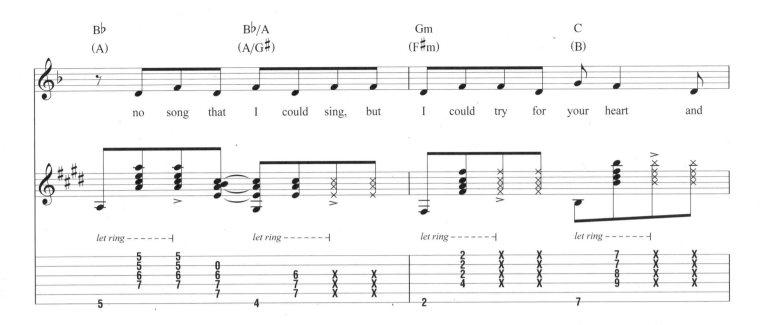

no song that I could sing, but I could try for your heart and

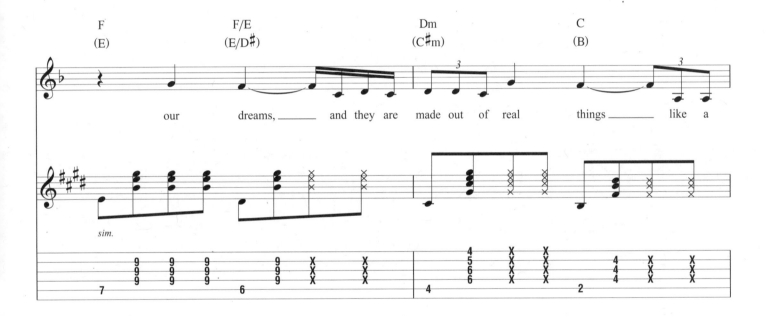

our dreams, _____ and they are made out of real things _____ like a

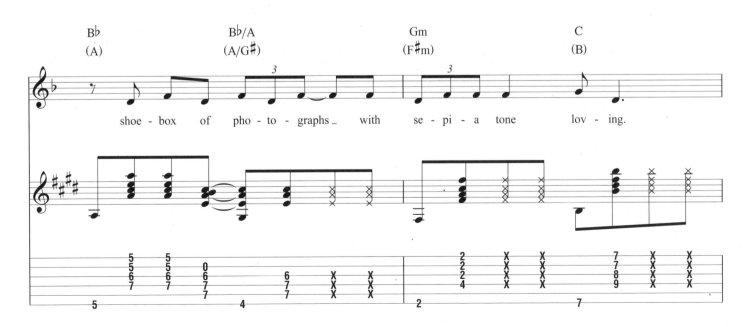

shoe - box of pho - to - graphs _ with se - pi - a tone lov - ing.

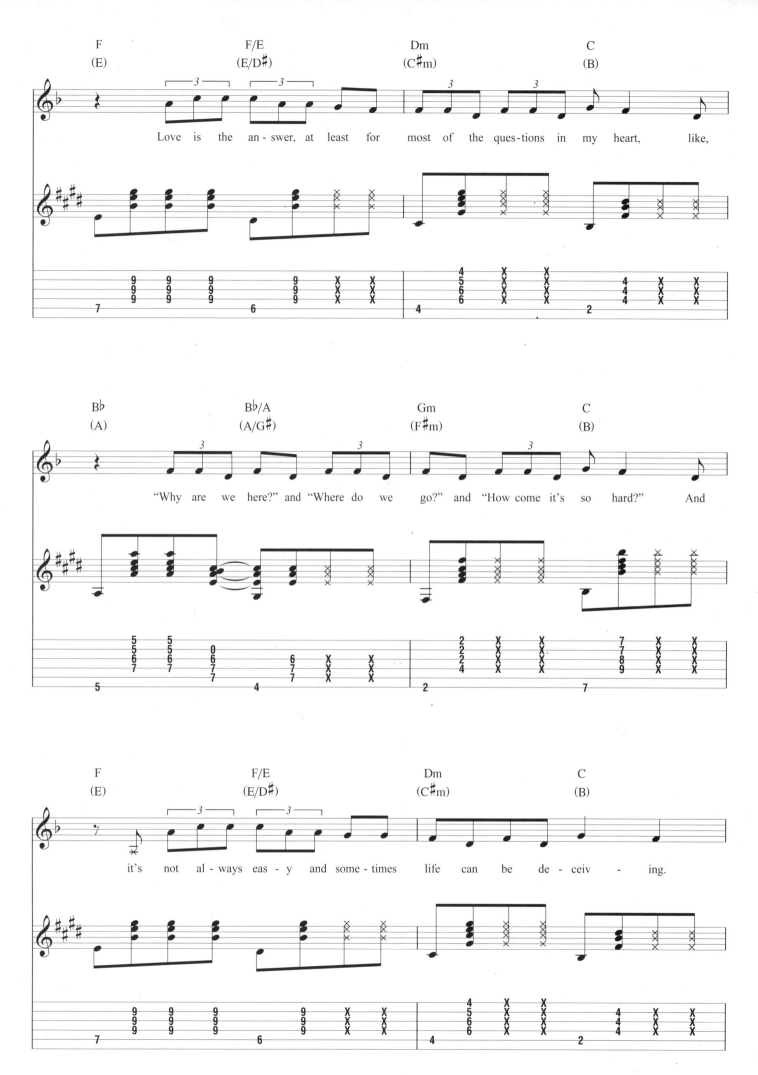

I'll tell you one thing, it's al - ways bet - ter when we're to - geth - er.

Chorus

Mm, ___ it's al - ways bet - ter when we're to - geth - er.

Yeah, ___ we'll look at the stars when we're to - geth - er.

Well, ___ it's al - ways bet - ter when we're to - geth - er.

Yeah, ___ it's al - ways bet - ter when we're to - geth - er. ___

Interlude

pret - ty sleep-ing next to me. But there is _____ not e - nough time. _

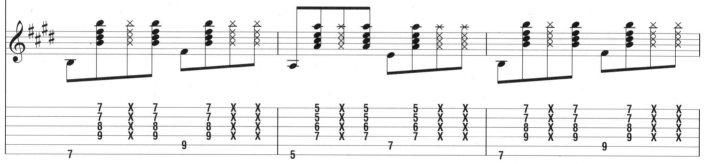

_____ _____ And there is no, _____ no song I could sing. _ And there is no _

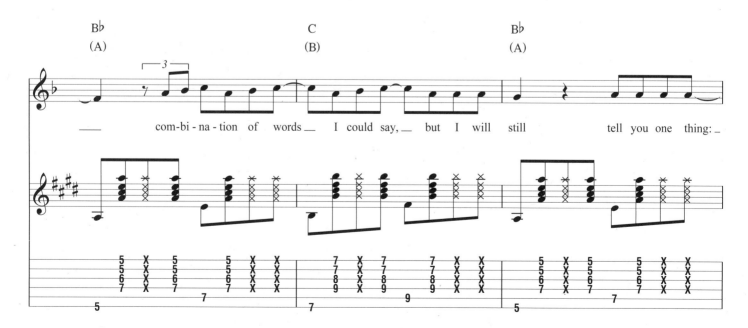

_ com - bi - na - tion of words _ I could say, _ but I will still tell you one thing: _

Outro

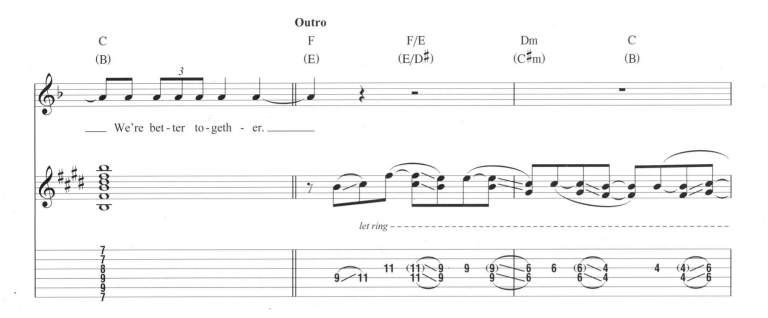

We're bet - ter to - geth - er.

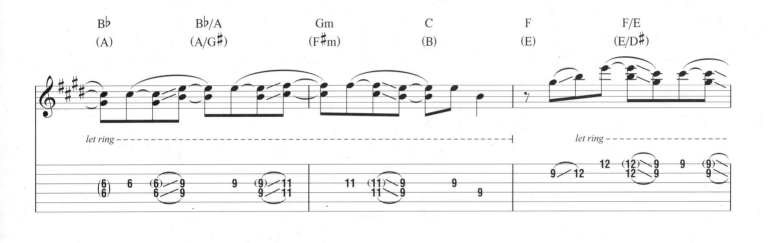

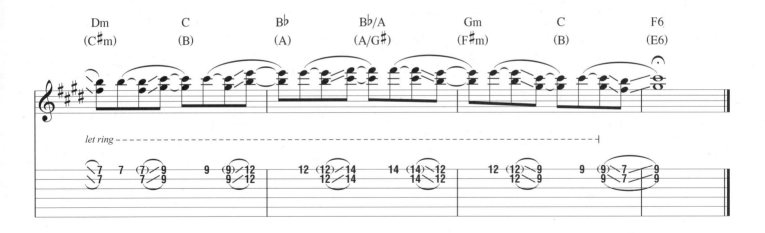

Additional Lyrics

2. And all of these moments just might find their way into my dreams tonight,
   But I know that they'll be gone when the morning light sings or brings new things.
   For tomorrow night you see that they'll be gone too; too many things I have to do.
   But if all of these dreams might find their way into my day-to-day scene,
   I'd be under the impression I was somewhere in between with only two,
   Just me and you, not so many things we got to do or places we got to be.
   We'll sit beneath the mango tree now.

Flake

Words and Music by Jack Johnson

Intro
Moderately ♩ = 98

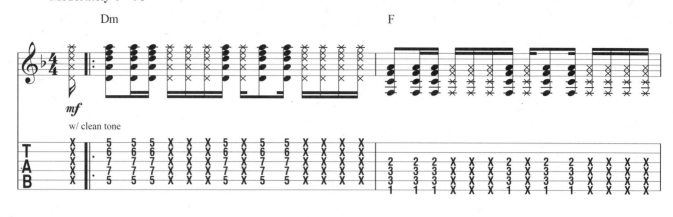

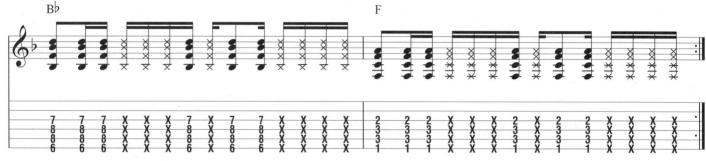

Verse

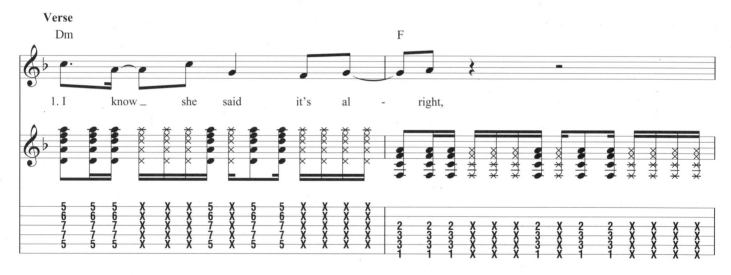

1. I know ___ she said it's al - right,

but you can make it up next time. _____

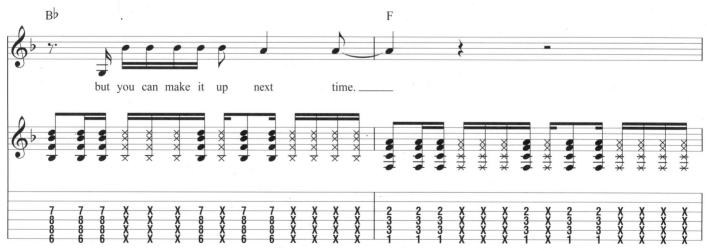

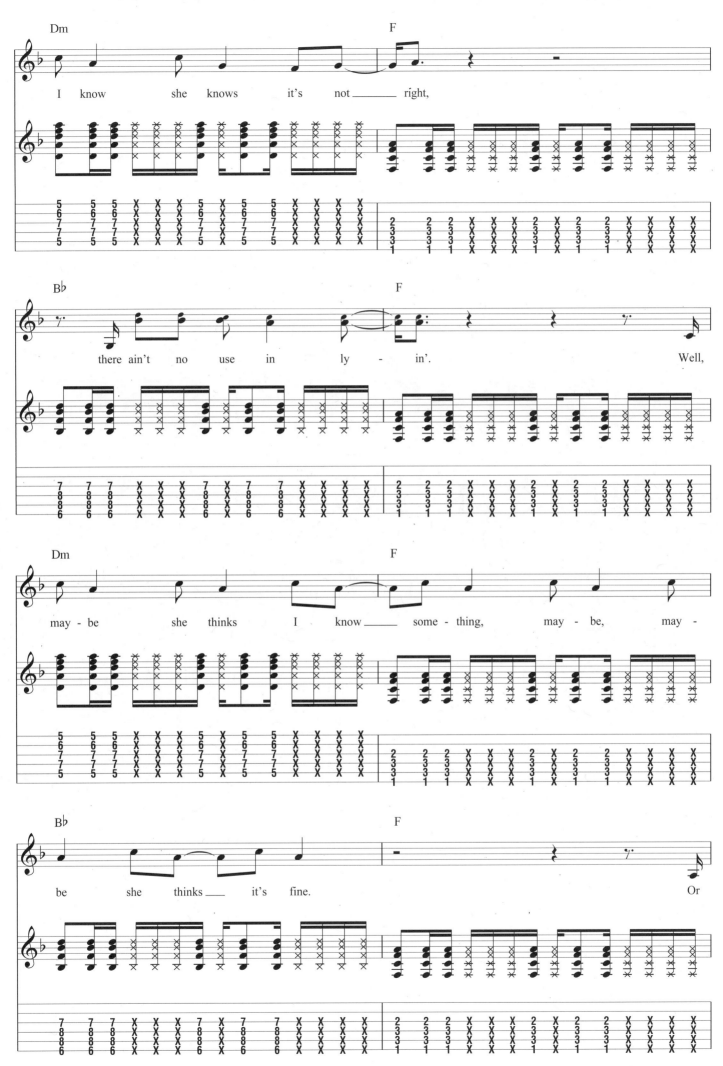

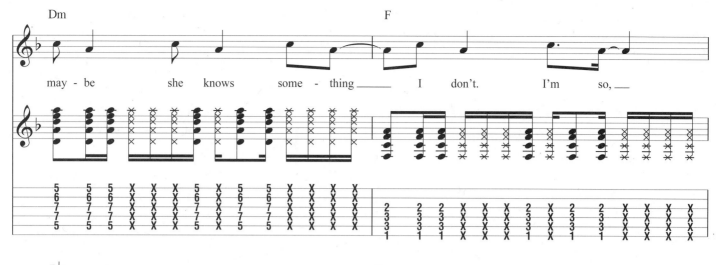

may-be she knows some-thing _____ I don't. I'm so, _____

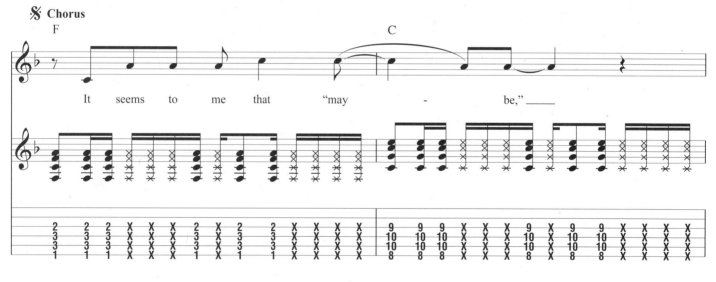

I'm so ti-red, I'm so ti-red of try-ing.

𝄋 Chorus

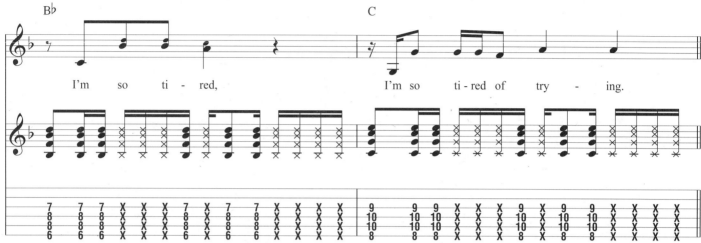

It seems to me that "may - be," _____

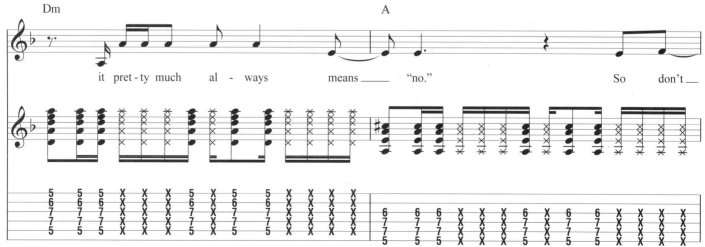

it pret-ty much al-ways means _____ "no." So don't _____

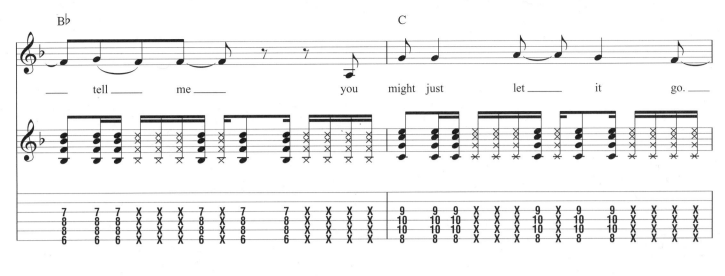

tell ___ me ___ you might just let ___ it go. ___

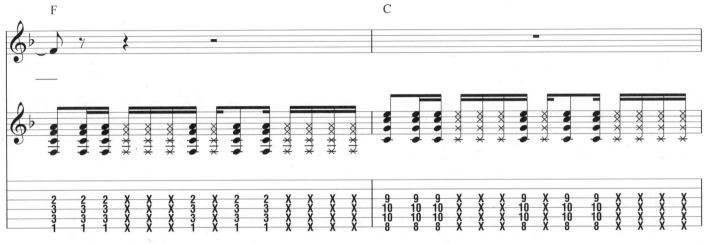

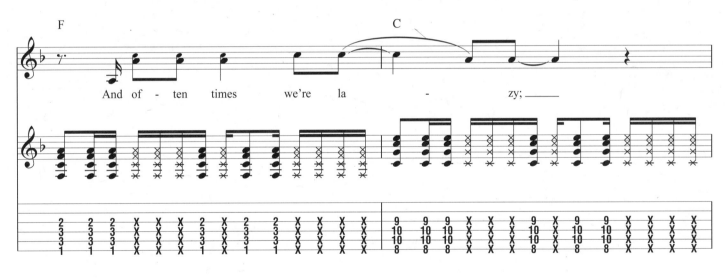

And of - ten times we're la - zy; ___

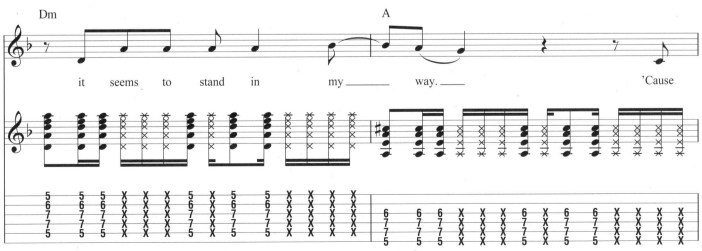

it seems to stand in my ___ way. ___ 'Cause

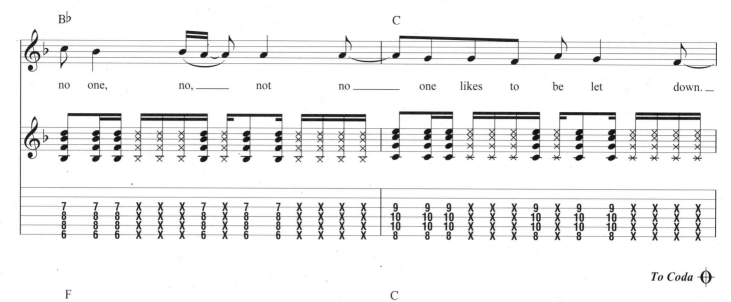

no one, no, ___ not no ___ one likes to be let down. ___

To Coda ⊕

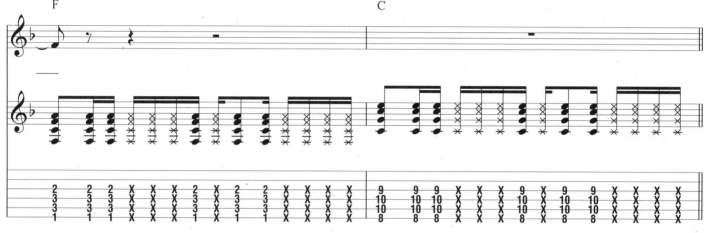

Verse

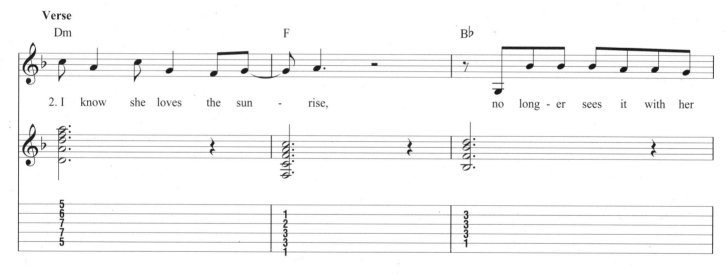

2. I know she loves the sun - rise, no long - er sees it with her

sleep - ing eyes ___ and... I know that when she said she's gon - na try, ___ well, it might

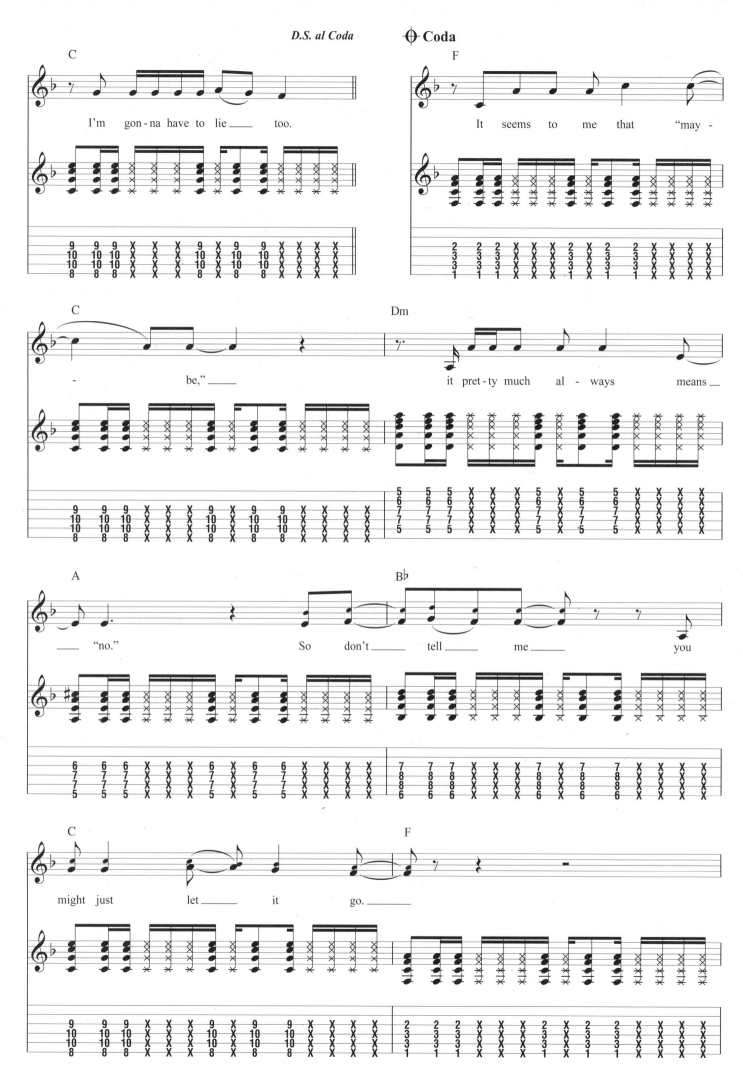

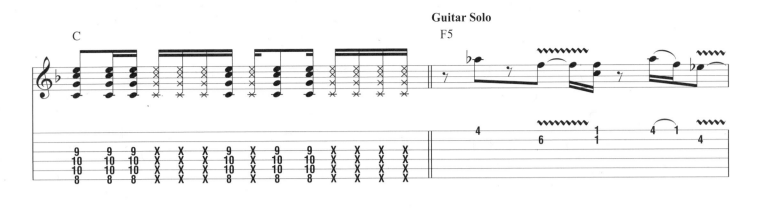

Guitar Solo

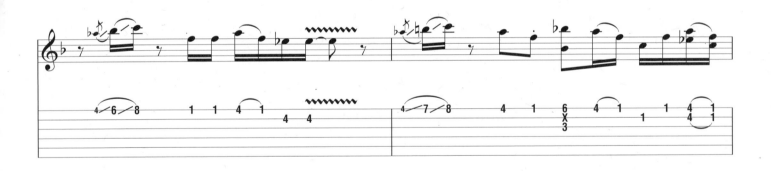

Outro

F5

Hard-er that you try, baby, the fur-ther you'll

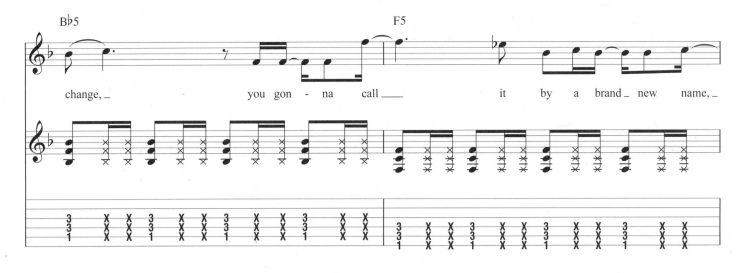

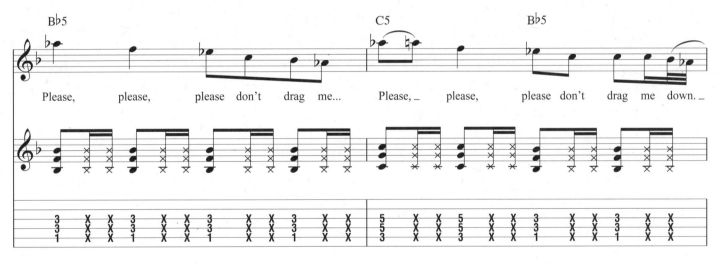

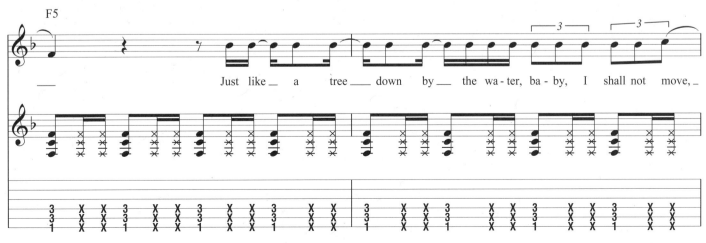

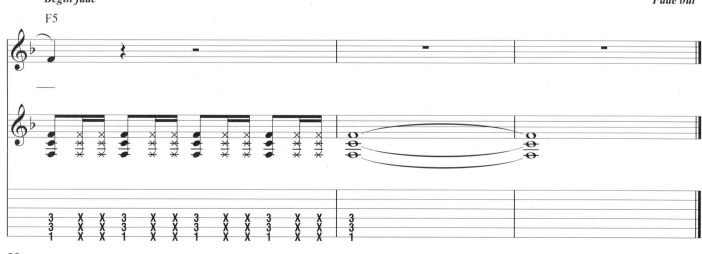

I Got You

Words and Music by Jack Johnson

Open C tuning, down 1/2 step:
(low to high) B-F♯-B-F♯-B-D♯

Intro
Moderately ♩ = 98

*Slap w/ thumb on lowest indicated string, downstroke w/ index finger on remaining strings.

1. Back when all ___

*Applies to harmonic pitches only.

take it on ___ for me. ___   When to - mor-row's too ___ much, I'll

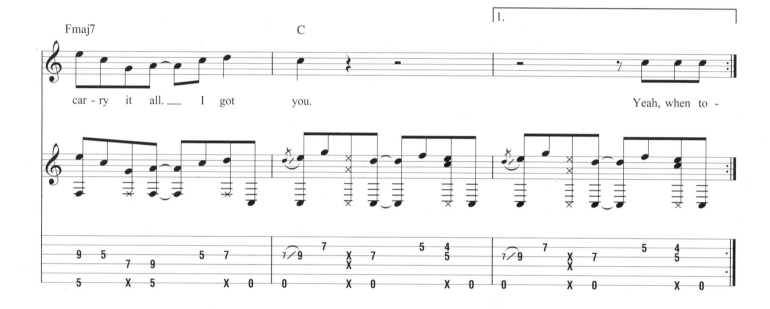

car - ry it all. ___ I got you.   Yeah, when to -

I got you.

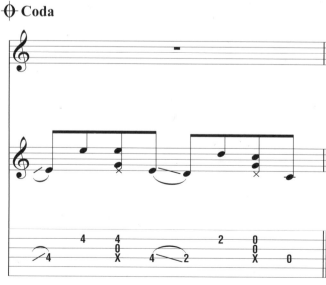

Outro

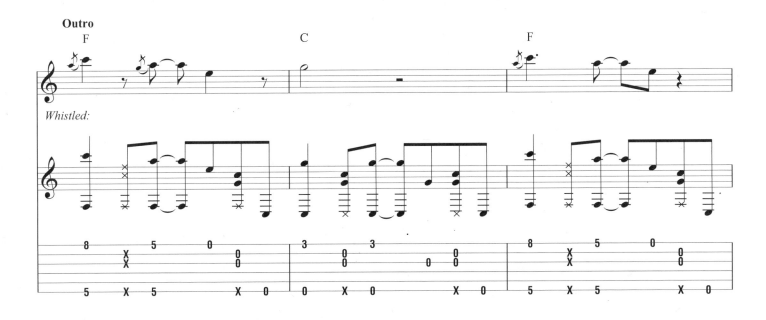

Whistled:

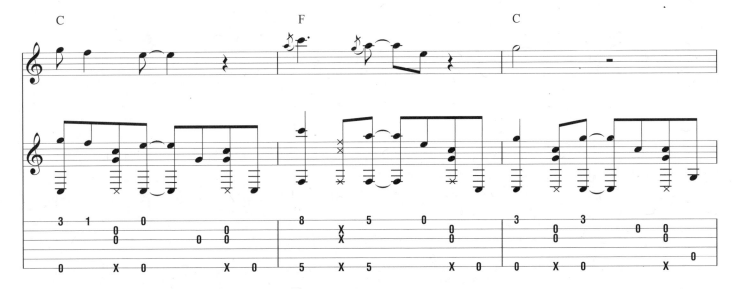

Additional Lyrics

2. We went walkin' through the hills try'n' to pretend that we both know.
   Maybe if we save up, we could build a little home.
   But then the hail storm came; it yelled, "You need to let it go. You got no control." No.

Good People

Words and Music by Jack Johnson

Intro
Moderately slow ♩ = 88

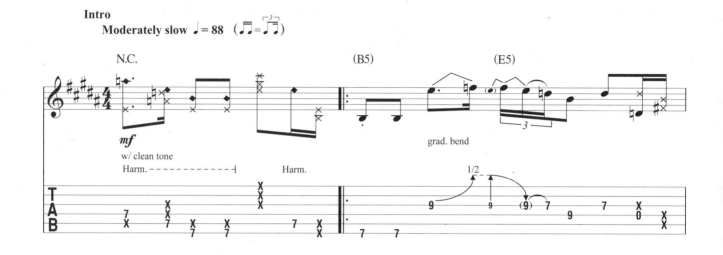

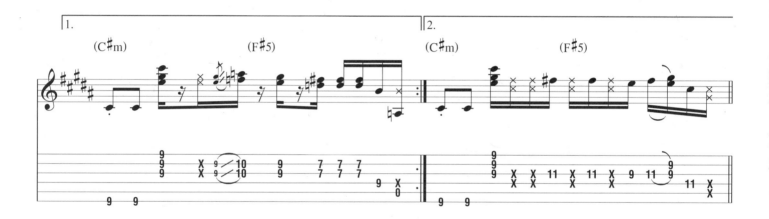

Verse

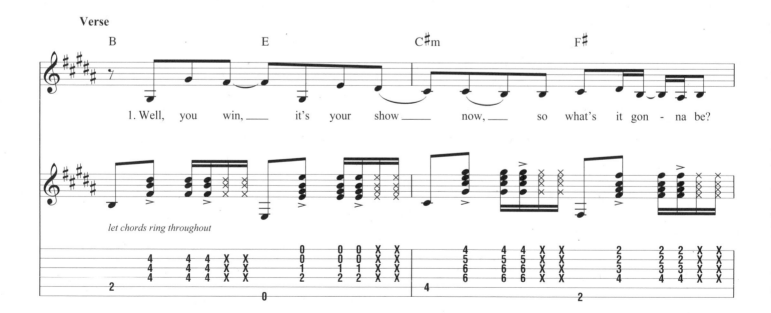

1. Well, you win, ___ it's your show ___ now, ___ so what's it gon - na be?

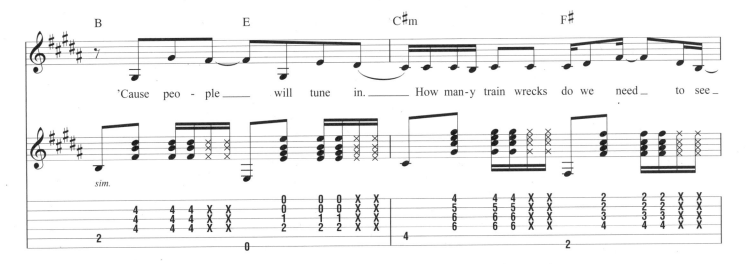

'Cause peo - ple ___ will tune in. ___ How man-y train wrecks do we need ___ to see ___

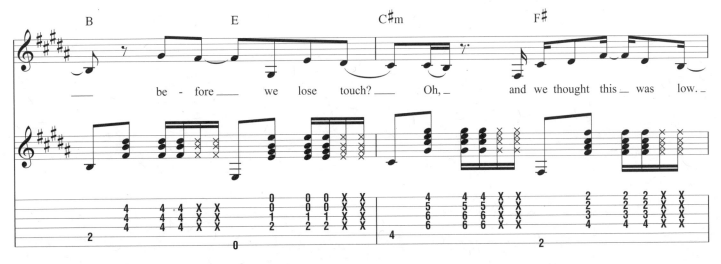

___ be - fore ___ we lose touch? ___ Oh, _ and we thought this _ was low. _

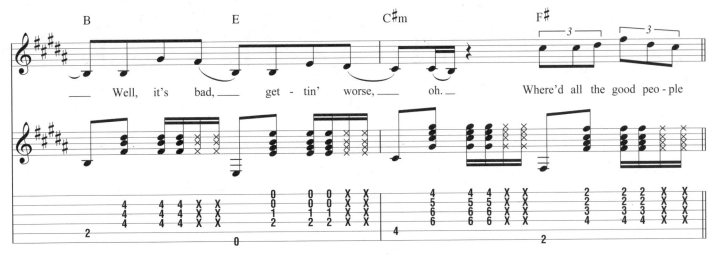

___ Well, it's bad, ___ get-tin' worse, ___ oh. ___ Where'd all the good peo - ple

𝄋 **Chorus**

go? ___ I've been chang-ing chan - nels; I don't ___

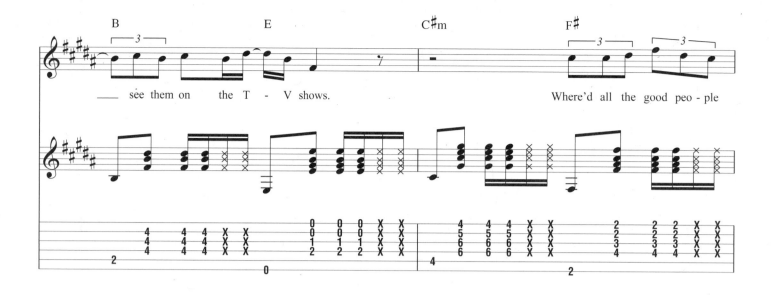

see them on the T - V shows.

Where'd all the good peo - ple

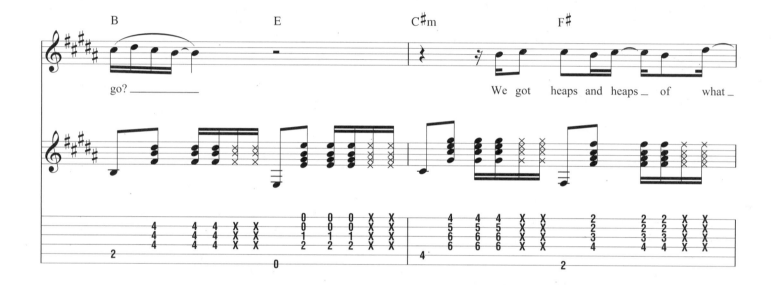

go? _____

We got heaps and heaps__ of what__

To Coda 1 ⊕
To Coda 2 ⊕

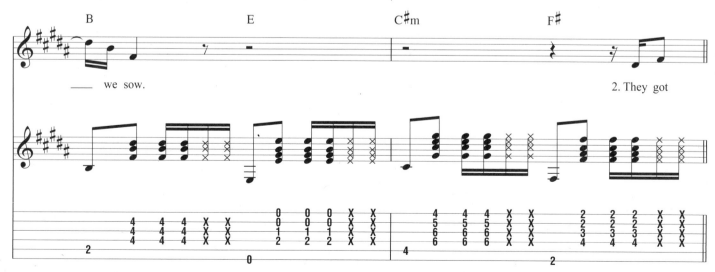

____ we sow.

2. They got

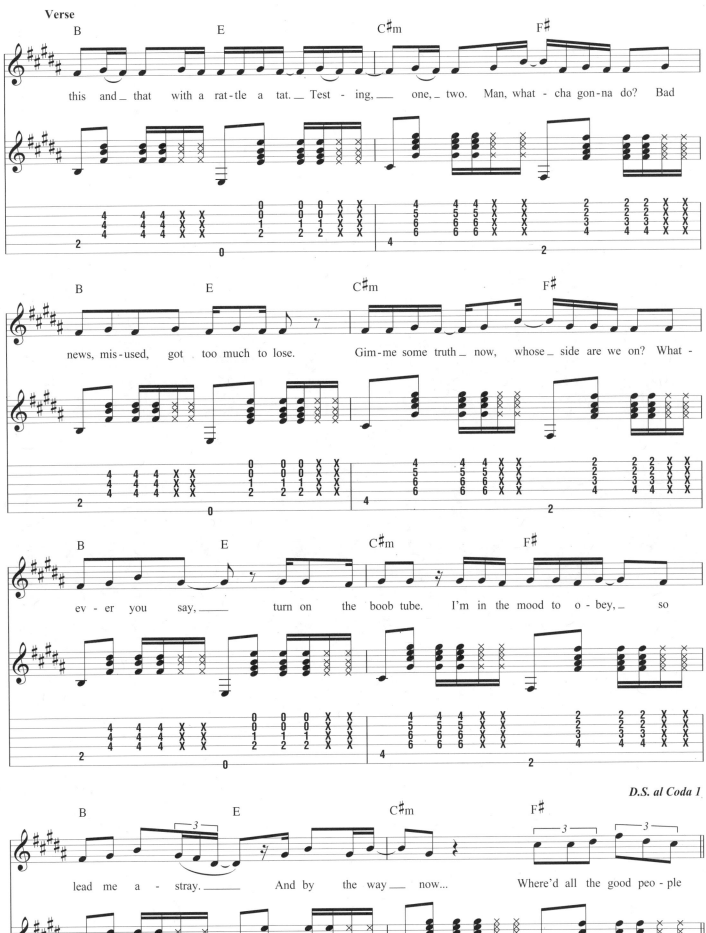

Coda 1

Interlude

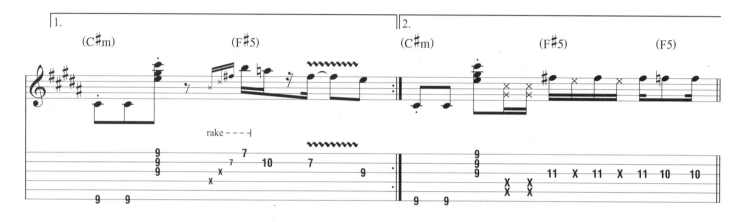

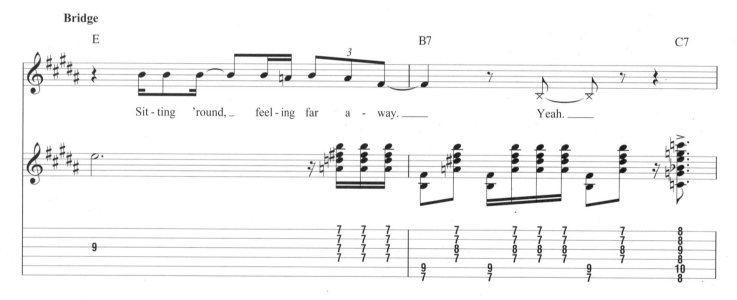

Bridge

Sit - ting 'round, _ feel - ing far a - way. _____ Yeah. _____

So far a - way, _ but I can feel the de - bris. Can you feel _ it?

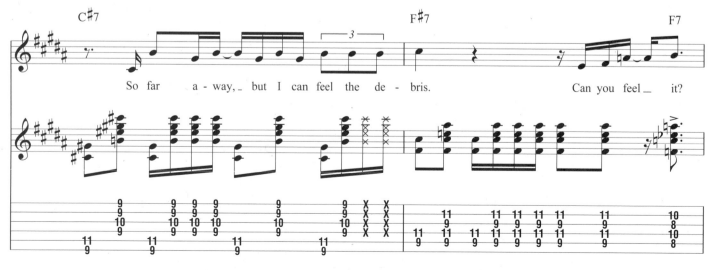

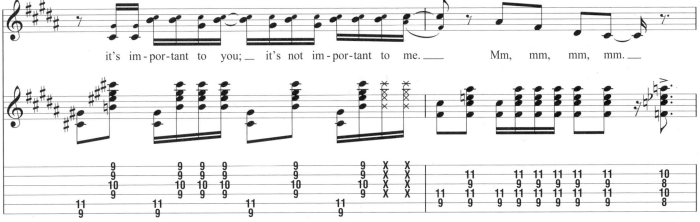

Way down by the edge of your ___ rea - son, ___

D.S. al Coda 2

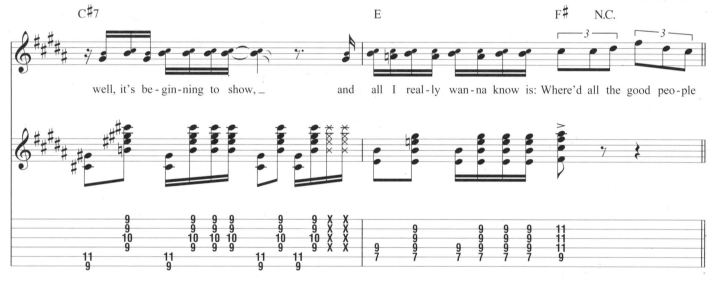

well, it's be - gin - ning to show, ___ and all I real - ly wan - na know is: Where'd all the good peo - ple

⊕ **Coda 2**

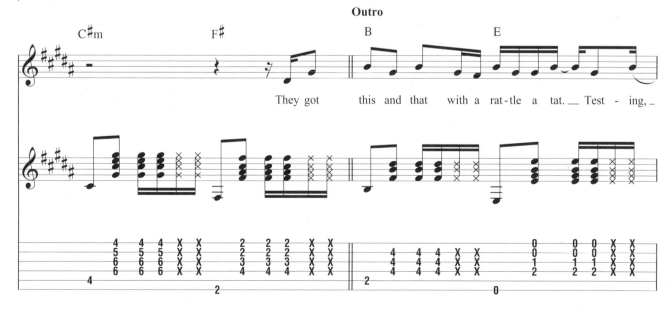

Outro

They got this and that with a rat - tle a tat. ___ Test - ing, ___

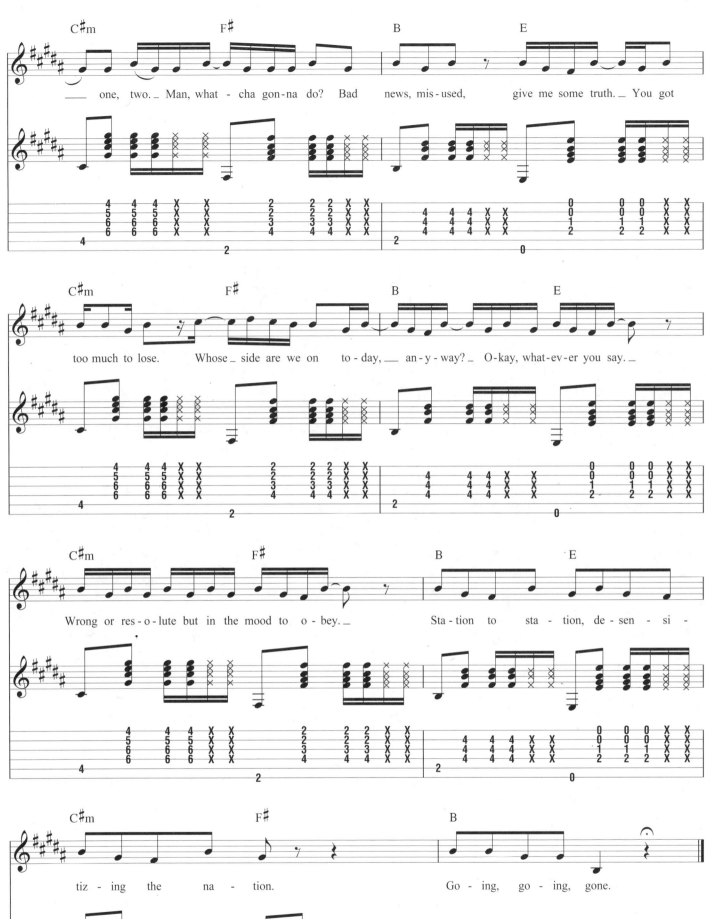

one, two._ Man, what-cha gon-na do? Bad news, mis-used, give me some truth._ You got

too much to lose. Whose_ side are we on to-day,_ an-y-way?_ O-kay, what-ev-er you say._

Wrong or res-o-lute but in the mood to o-bey._ Sta-tion to sta-tion, de-sen-si-

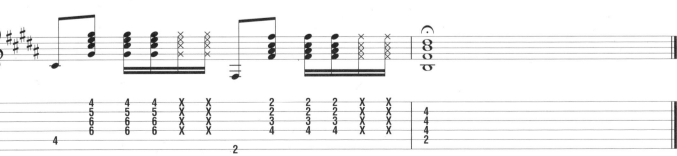

tiz-ing the na-tion. Go-ing, go-ing, gone.

If I Had Eyes

Words and Music by Jack Johnson

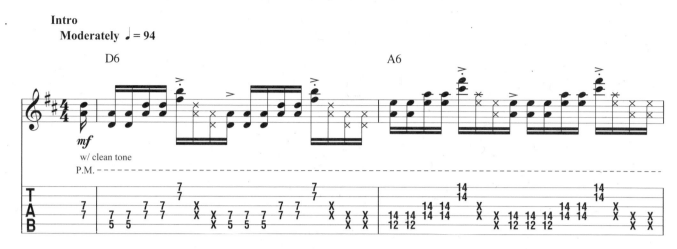

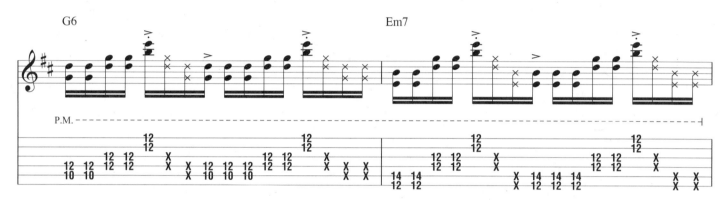

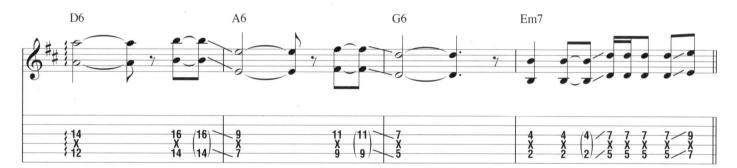

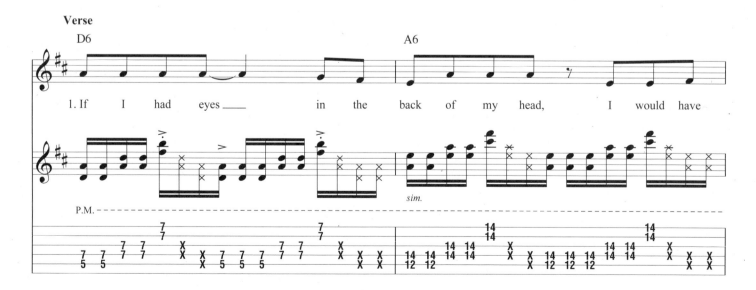

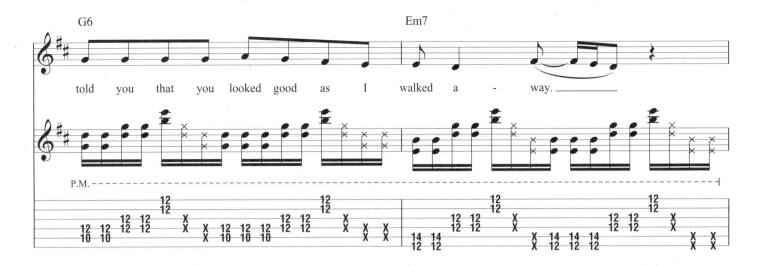

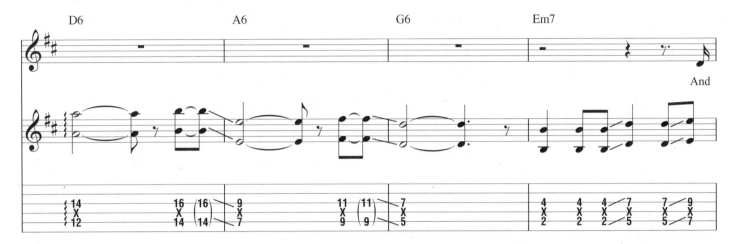

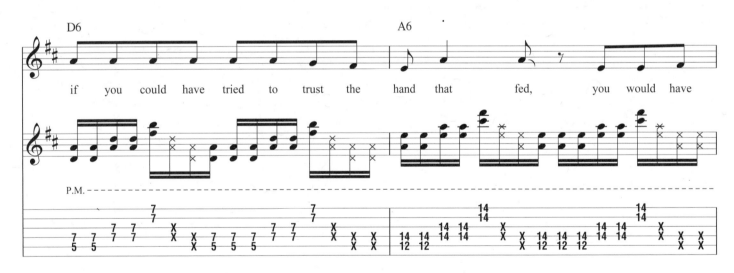

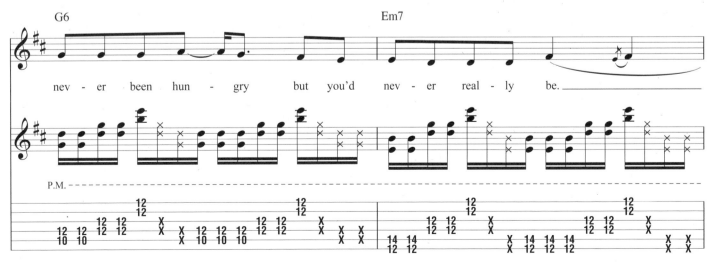

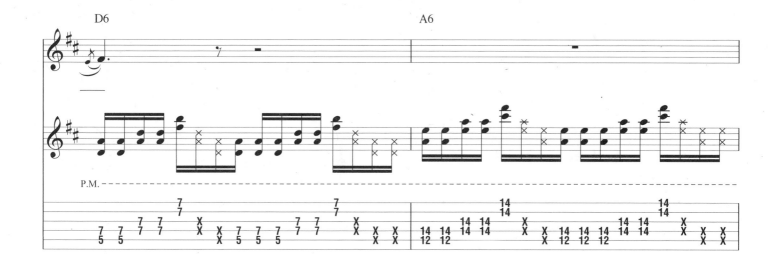

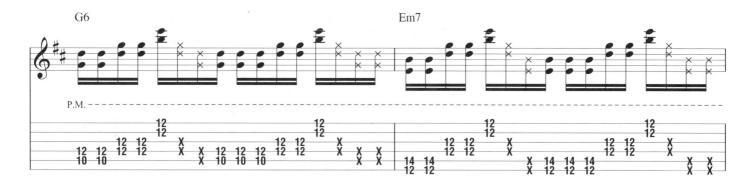

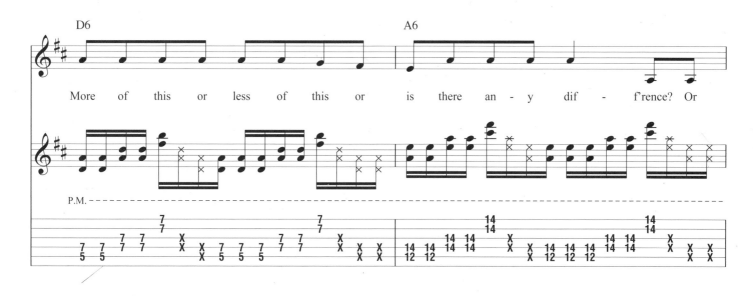

More of this or less of this or is there an - y dif - f'rence? Or

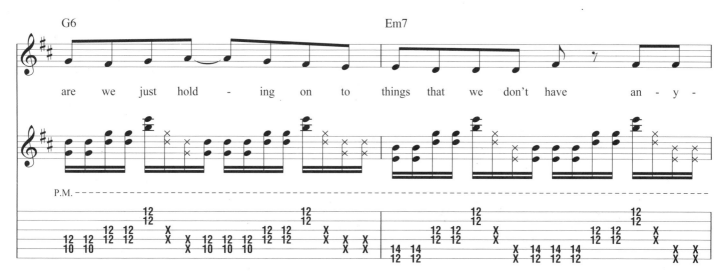

are we just hold - ing on to things that we don't have an - y-

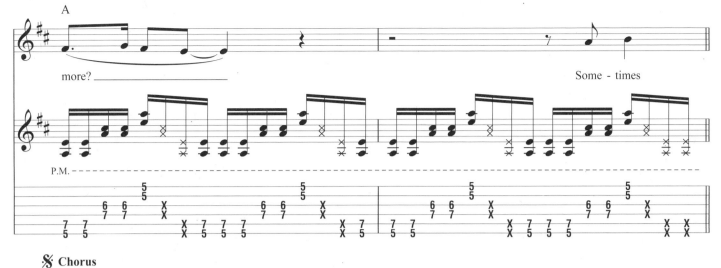

more? _____ Some - times

% Chorus

time does - n't heal. _____ No, not _ at all. _____ It

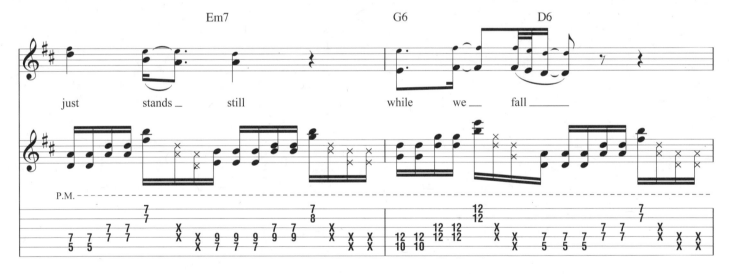

just stands _ still while we _ fall _____ in or out _____ of love a - gain. I _____ doubt _____ I'm gon - na

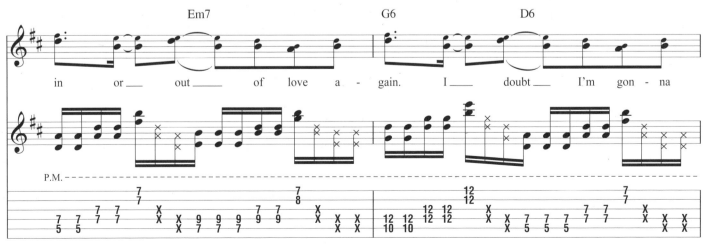

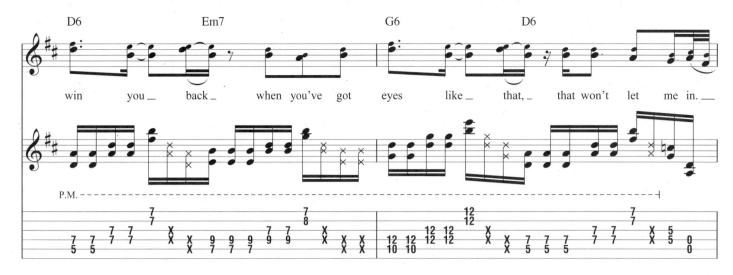

win you _ back _ when you've got eyes like _ that, _ that won't let me in. _

To Coda ⊕

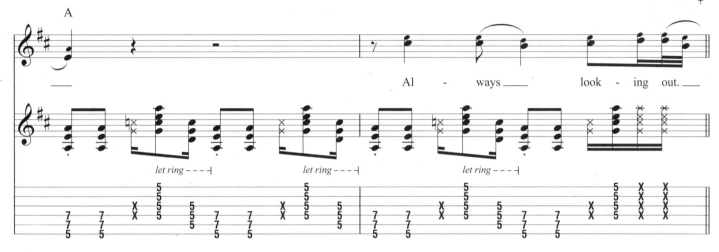

_ Al - ways _ look - ing out. _

Interlude

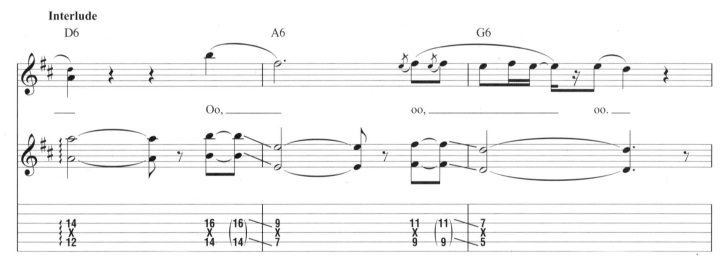

Oo, _ oo, _ oo. _

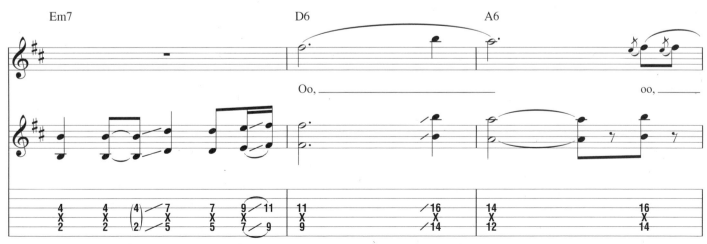

Oo, _ oo, _

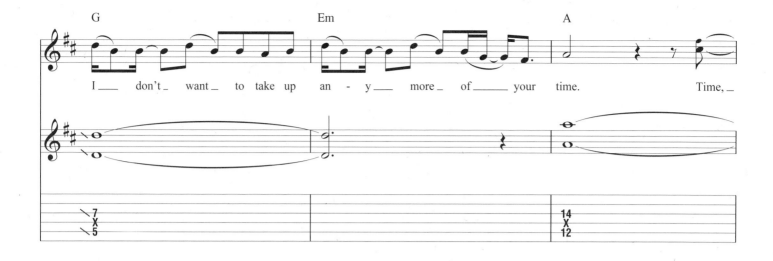

I___ don't___ want___ to take up an - y___ more___ of_____ your time.

Time, ___

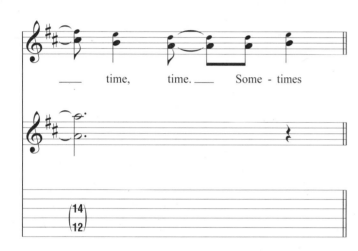

___ time, time.___ Some - times

D.S. al Coda

⊕ Coda

Outro

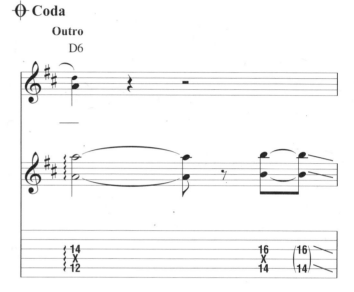

___

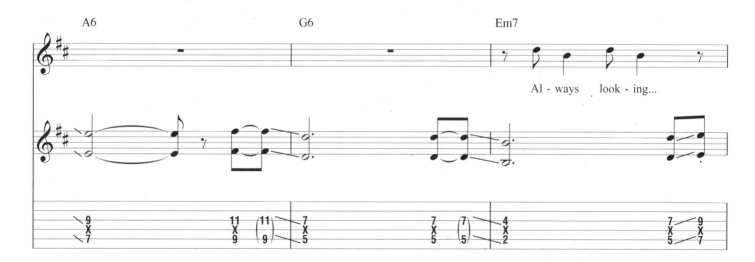

Al - ways look - ing...

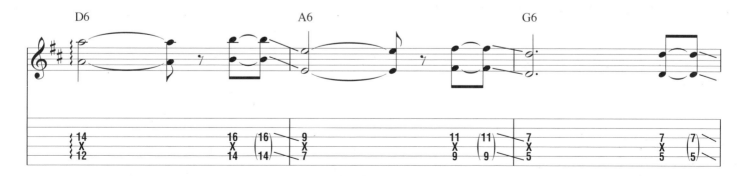

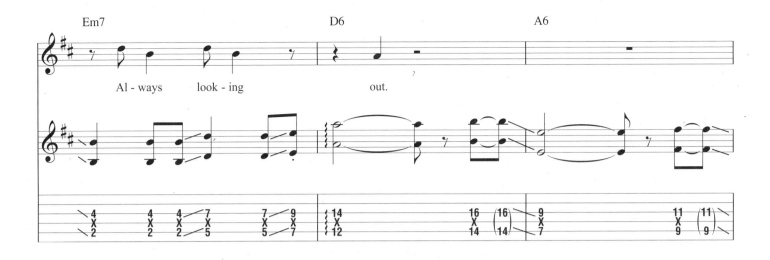

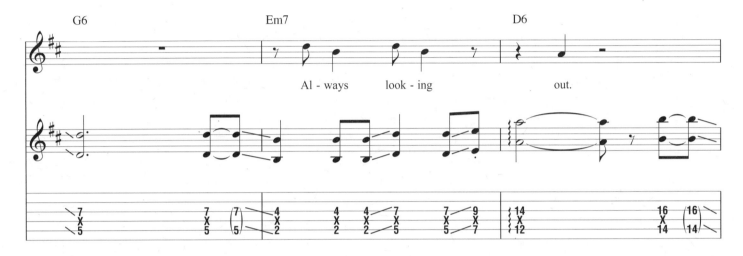

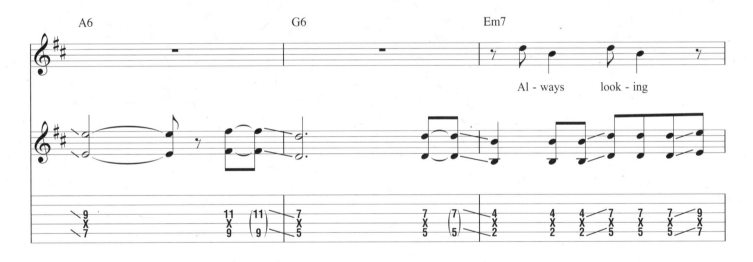

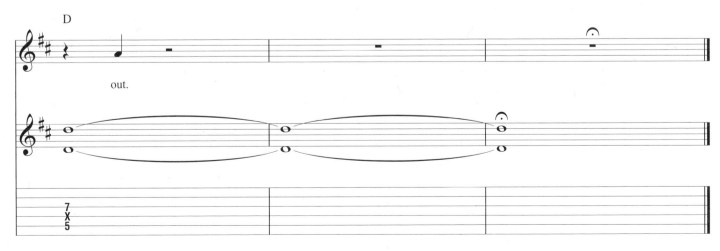

Sitting, Waiting, Wishing

Words and Music by Jack Johnson

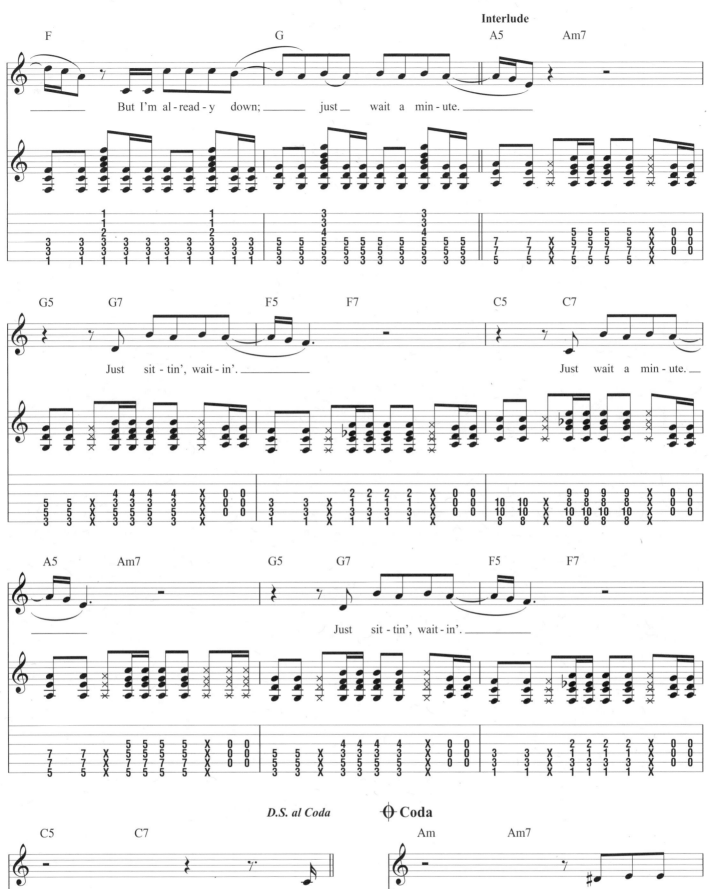

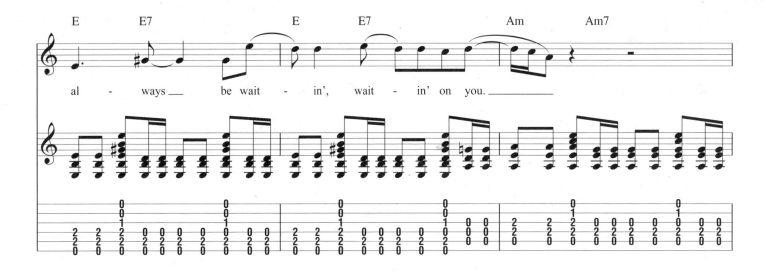

al - ways ___ be wait - in', wait - in' on you. ___

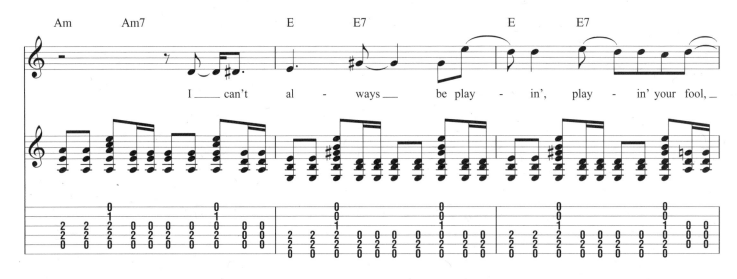

I ___ can't al - ways ___ be play - in', play - in' your fool, ___

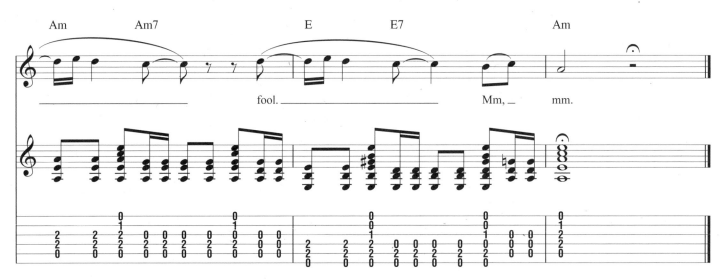

___ fool. ___ Mm, ___ mm.

Additional Lyrics

2. I sang your songs, I danced your dance, I gave your friends all a chance.
   Puttin' up with them wasn't worth never havin' you.
   Oh, maybe you've been through this before, but it's my first time,
   So please ignore the next few lines 'cause they're directed at you.

3. Well, if I was in your position I'd put down all my ammunition.
   I'd wonder why it had taken me so long.
   But Lord knows that I'm not you, and if I was, I wouldn't be so cruel,
   'Cause waitin' on love ain't so easy to do.

You and Your Heart

Words and Music by Jack Johnson

Verse

1. Watch you when you say what you are and when you blame ev'ry-
2. *See additional lyrics*

one,_____ you bro - ken king._____

Watch you change the frame, I'll watch you when you take your aim at the

sum _____ of ev'ry - thing. _____ But

50

Interlude

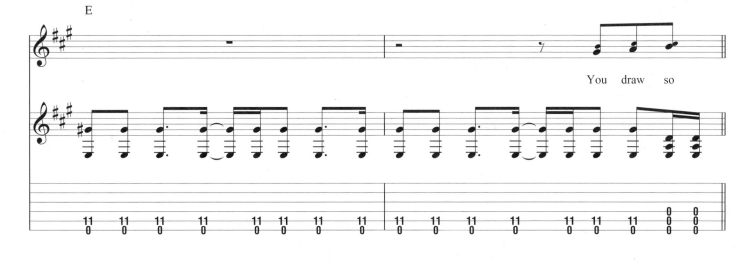

Outro

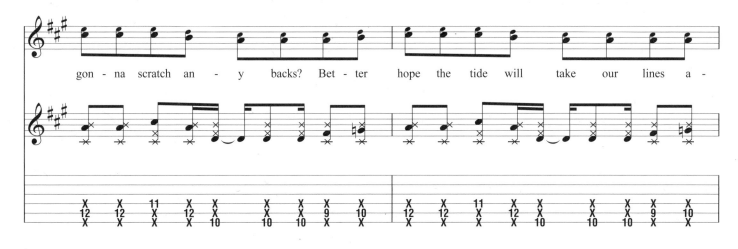

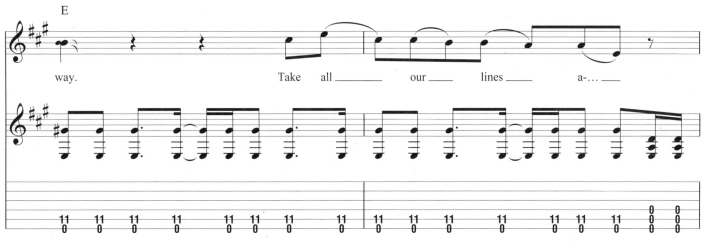

Hope the tide will take our lines a-...

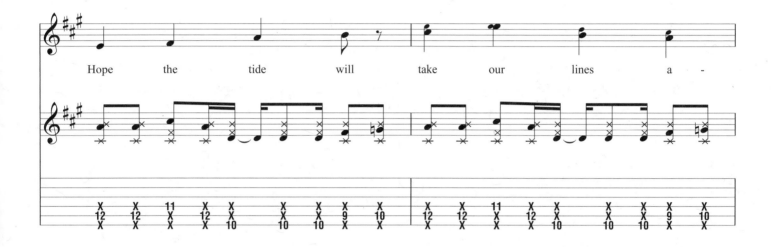

Hope the tide will take our lines a -

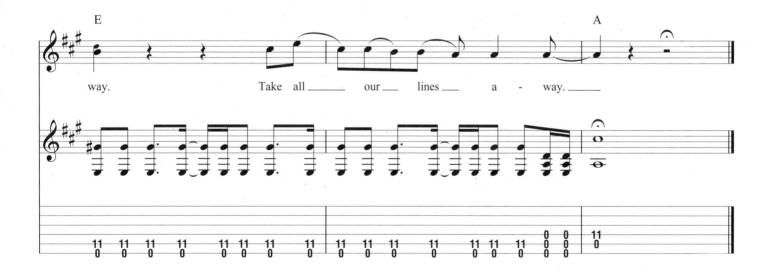

way. Take all our lines a - way.

Additional Lyrics

2. Lay there in the street like broken glass reflecting pieces of the sun,
   But you're not the flame.
   You cut the people passing by because you know what you don't like.
   It's just so easy. It's just so easy.

Upside Down

from the Universal Pictures and Imagine Entertainment film CURIOUS GEORGE

Words and Music by Jack Johnson

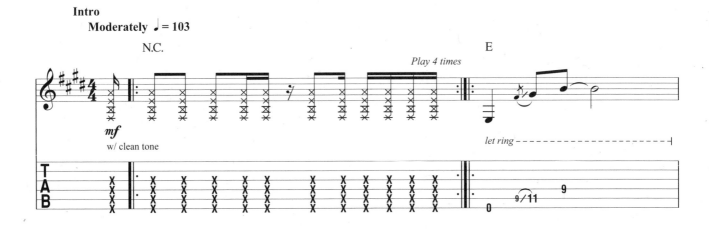

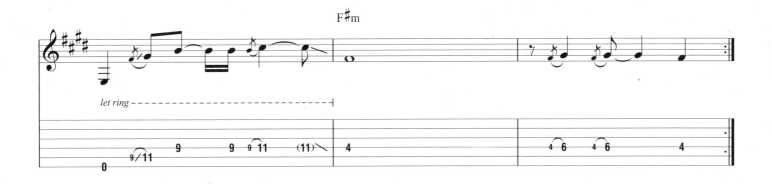

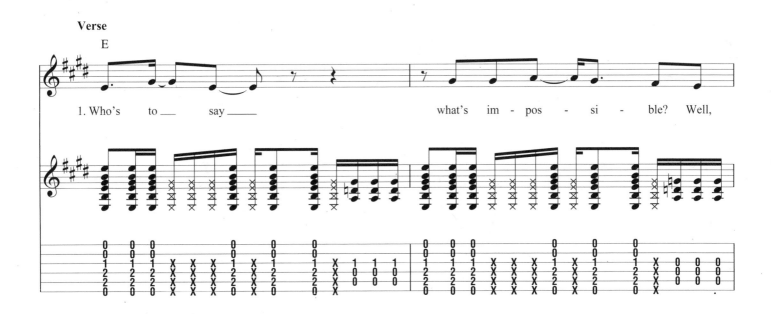

they for - got _____ this world keeps spin-nin'. And _ with

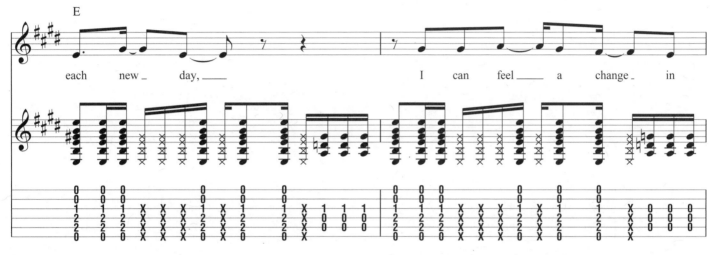

each new _ day, _____ I can feel _____ a change _ in

ev - 'ry - thing. _____ And as the sur - face breaks, re -

flec - tions _ fade, _____ but in some _____ ways _ they re -

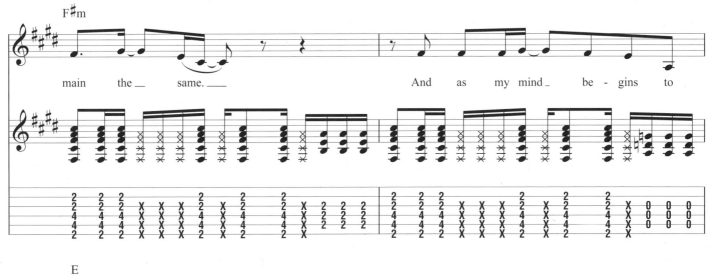

main the __ same. __ And as my mind __ be - gins to

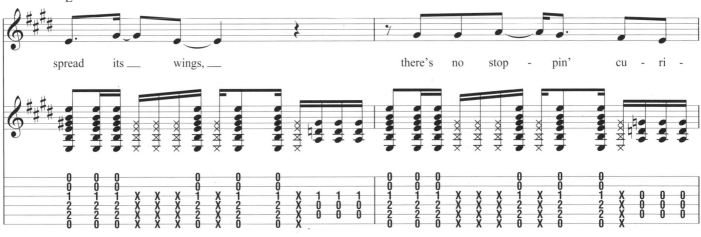

spread its __ wings, __ there's no stop - pin' cu - ri -

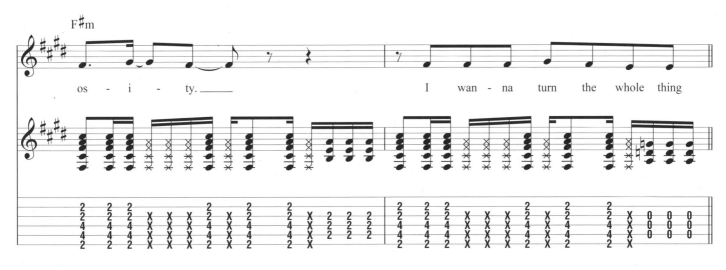

os - i - ty. _____ I wan - na turn the whole thing

𝄋 **Chorus**

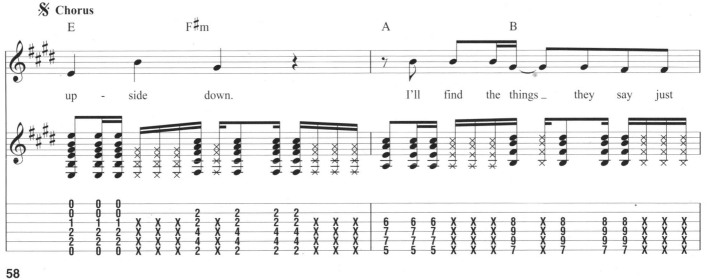

up - side down. I'll find the things __ they say just

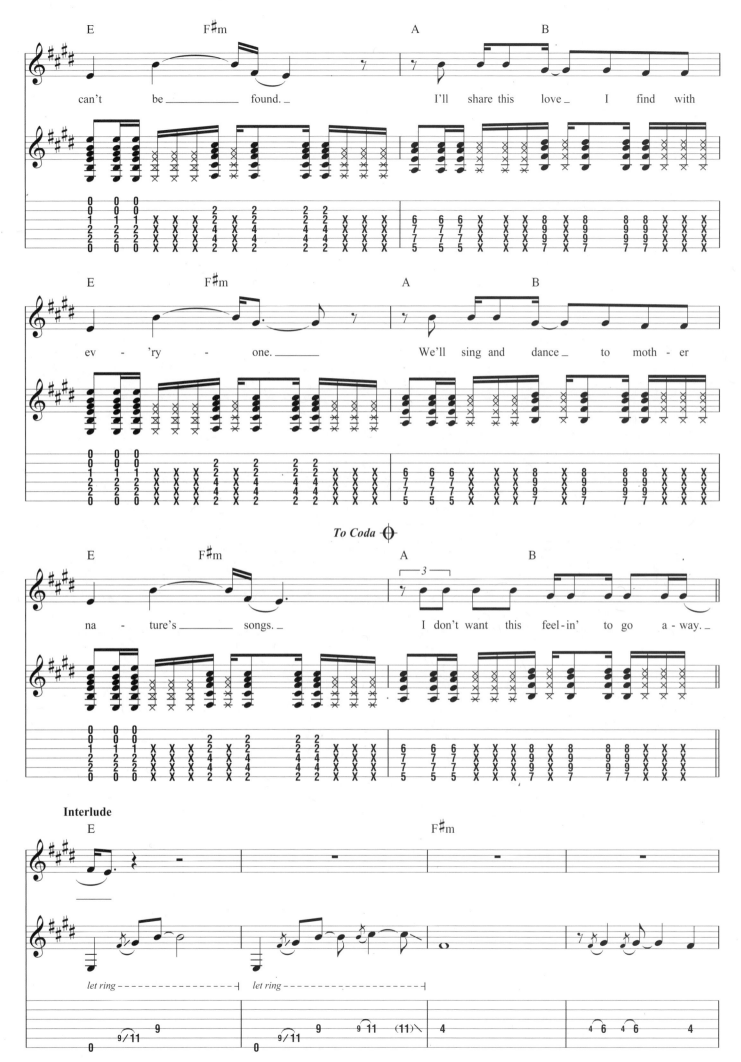

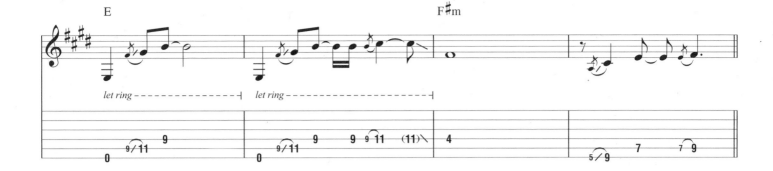

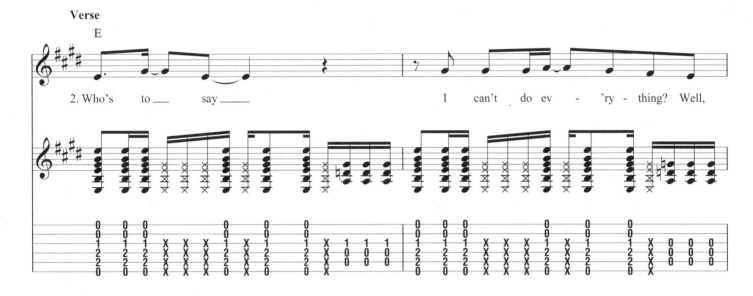

Verse

2. Who's to ___ say ___ I can't do ev - 'ry - thing? Well,

I can ___ try. ___ And as I roll a - long ___ I be -

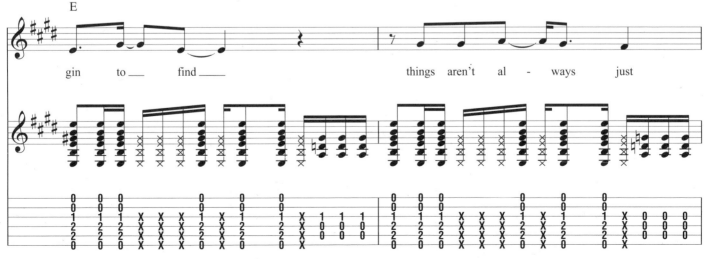

gin to ___ find ___ things aren't al - ways just

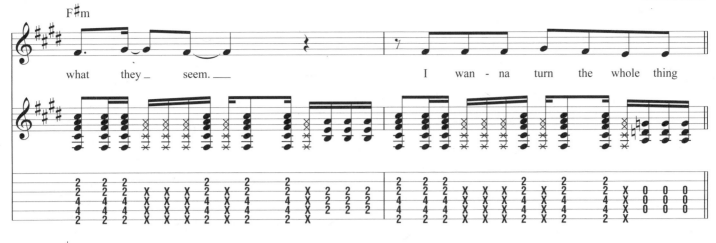

what they _ seem. _____   I wan - na turn the whole thing

Coda

Bridge

This world keeps spin - nin' and _ there's   no   time to waste. _

_____   Well, it all _____   keeps

Chorus

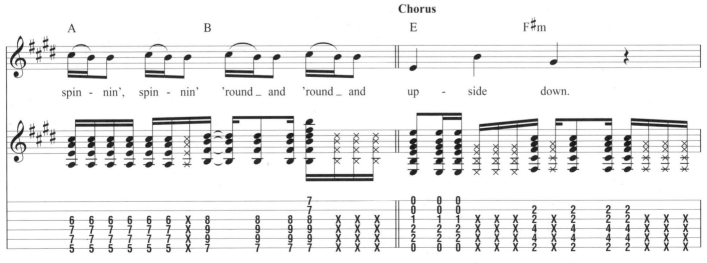

spin - nin', spin - nin' 'round _ and 'round _ and   up - side down.

Please _ don't go a - way. ____

Slower ♩ = 82

Is this how it's sup-posed. to be? _____ Is

this how it's sup - posed to be? _____

HAL·LEONARD GUITAR PLAY-ALONG

This series will help you play your favorite songs quickly and easily. Just follow the tab and listen to the CD to the hear how the guitar should sound, and then play along using the separate backing tracks. Mac or PC users can also slow down the tempo without changing pitch by using the CD in their computer. The melody and lyrics are included in the book so that you can sing or simply follow along.

INCLUDES TAB

VOL. 1 – ROCK	00699570 / $16.99
VOL. 2 – ACOUSTIC	00699569 / $16.95
VOL. 3 – HARD ROCK	00699573 / $16.95
VOL. 4 – POP/ROCK	00699571 / $16.99
VOL. 5 – MODERN ROCK	00699574 / $16.99
VOL. 6 – '90S ROCK	00699572 / $16.99
VOL. 7 – BLUES	00699575 / $16.95
VOL. 8 – ROCK	00699585 / $14.99
VOL. 9 – PUNK ROCK	00699576 / $14.95
VOL. 10 – ACOUSTIC	00699586 / $16.95
VOL. 11 – EARLY ROCK	00699579 / $14.95
VOL. 12 – POP/ROCK	00699587 / $14.95
VOL. 13 – FOLK ROCK	00699581 / $15.99
VOL. 14 – BLUES ROCK	00699582 / $16.95
VOL. 15 – R&B	00699583 / $14.95
VOL. 16 – JAZZ	00699584 / $15.95
VOL. 17 – COUNTRY	00699588 / $15.95
VOL. 18 – ACOUSTIC ROCK	00699577 / $15.95
VOL. 19 – SOUL	00699578 / $14.99
VOL. 20 – ROCKABILLY	00699580 / $14.95
VOL. 21 – YULETIDE	00699602 / $14.95
VOL. 22 – CHRISTMAS	00699600 / $15.95
VOL. 23 – SURF	00699635 / $14.95
VOL. 24 – ERIC CLAPTON	00699649 / $17.99
VOL. 25 – LENNON & MCCARTNEY	00699642 / $16.99
VOL. 26 – ELVIS PRESLEY	00699643 / $14.95
VOL. 27 – DAVID LEE ROTH	00699645 / $16.95
VOL. 28 – GREG KOCH	00699646 / $14.95
VOL. 29 – BOB SEGER	00699647 / $15.99
VOL. 30 – KISS	00699644 / $16.99
VOL. 31 – CHRISTMAS HITS	00699652 / $14.95
VOL. 32 – THE OFFSPRING	00699653 / $14.95
VOL. 33 – ACOUSTIC CLASSICS	00699656 / $16.95
VOL. 34 – CLASSIC ROCK	00699658 / $16.95
VOL. 35 – HAIR METAL	00699660 / $16.95
VOL. 36 – SOUTHERN ROCK	00699661 / $16.95
VOL. 37 – ACOUSTIC UNPLUGGED	00699662 / $22.99
VOL. 38 – BLUES	00699663 / $16.95
VOL. 39 – '80S METAL	00699664 / $16.99
VOL. 40 – INCUBUS	00699668 / $17.95
VOL. 41 – ERIC CLAPTON	00699669 / $16.95
VOL. 42 – 2000S ROCK	00699670 / $16.99
VOL. 43 – LYNYRD SKYNYRD	00699681 / $17.95
VOL. 44 – JAZZ	00699689 / $14.99
VOL. 45 – TV THEMES	00699718 / $14.95
VOL. 46 – MAINSTREAM ROCK	00699722 / $16.95
VOL. 47 – HENDRIX SMASH HITS	00699723 / $19.95
VOL. 48 – AEROSMITH CLASSICS	00699724 / $17.99
VOL. 49 – STEVIE RAY VAUGHAN	00699725 / $17.99
VOL. 51 – ALTERNATIVE '90S	00699727 / $14.99
VOL. 52 – FUNK	00699728 / $14.95
VOL. 53 – DISCO	00699729 / $14.99
VOL. 54 – HEAVY METAL	00699730 / $14.95
VOL. 55 – POP METAL	00699731 / $14.95
VOL. 56 – FOO FIGHTERS	00699749 / $15.99
VOL. 57 – SYSTEM OF A DOWN	00699751 / $14.95
VOL. 58 – BLINK-182	00699772 / $14.95

VOL. 59 – CHET ATKINS	00702347 / $16.99
VOL. 60 – 3 DOORS DOWN	00699774 / $14.95
VOL. 61 – SLIPKNOT	00699775 / $16.99
VOL. 62 – CHRISTMAS CAROLS	00699798 / $12.95
VOL. 63 – CREEDENCE CLEARWATER REVIVAL	00699802 / $16.99
VOL. 64 – THE ULTIMATE OZZY OSBOURNE	00699803 / $16.99
VOL. 66 – THE ROLLING STONES	00699807 / $16.95
VOL. 67 – BLACK SABBATH	00699808 / $16.99
VOL. 68 – PINK FLOYD – DARK SIDE OF THE MOON	00699809 / $16.99
VOL. 69 – ACOUSTIC FAVORITES	00699810 / $14.95
VOL. 70 – OZZY OSBOURNE	00699805 / $16.99
VOL. 71 – CHRISTIAN ROCK	00699824 / $14.95
VOL. 73 – BLUESY ROCK	00699829 / $16.99
VOL. 75 – TOM PETTY	00699882 / $16.99
VOL. 76 – COUNTRY HITS	00699884 / $14.95
VOL. 77 – BLUEGRASS	00699910 / $14.99
VOL. 78 – NIRVANA	00700132 / $16.99
VOL. 79 – NEIL YOUNG	00700133 / $24.99
VOL. 80 – ACOUSTIC ANTHOLOGY	00700175 / $19.95
VOL. 81 – ROCK ANTHOLOGY	00700176 / $22.99
VOL. 82 – EASY SONGS	00700177 / $12.99
VOL. 83 – THREE CHORD SONGS	00700178 / $16.99
VOL. 84 – STEELY DAN	00700200 / $16.99
VOL. 85 – THE POLICE	00700269 / $16.99
VOL. 86 – BOSTON	00700465 / $16.99
VOL. 87 – ACOUSTIC WOMEN	00700763 / $14.99
VOL. 88 – GRUNGE	00700467 / $16.99
VOL. 89 – REGGAE	00700468 / $15.99
VOL. 90 – CLASSICAL POP	00700469 / $14.99
VOL. 91 – BLUES INSTRUMENTALS	00700505 / $14.99
VOL. 92 – EARLY ROCK INSTRUMENTALS	00700506 / $14.99
VOL. 93 – ROCK INSTRUMENTALS	00700507 / $16.99
VOL. 95 – BLUES CLASSICS	00700509 / $14.99
VOL. 96 – THIRD DAY	00700560 / $14.95
VOL. 97 – ROCK BAND	00700703 / $14.99
VOL. 99 – ZZ TOP	00700762 / $16.99
VOL. 100 – B.B. KING	00700466 / $16.99
VOL. 101 – SONGS FOR BEGINNERS	00701917 / $14.99
VOL. 102 – CLASSIC PUNK	00700769 / $14.99
VOL. 103 – SWITCHFOOT	00700773 / $16.99
VOL. 104 – DUANE ALLMAN	00700846 / $16.99
VOL. 106 – WEEZER	00700958 / $14.99
VOL. 107 – CREAM	00701069 / $16.99
VOL. 108 – THE WHO	00701053 / $16.99
VOL. 109 – STEVE MILLER	00701054 / $14.99
VOL. 111 – JOHN MELLENCAMP	00701056 / $14.99
VOL. 112 – QUEEN	00701052 / $16.99
VOL. 113 – JIM CROCE	00701058 / $15.99
VOL. 114 – BON JOVI	00701060 / $14.99
VOL. 115 – JOHNNY CASH	00701070 / $16.99
VOL. 116 – THE VENTURES	00701124 / $14.99
VOL. 117 – BRAD PAISLEY	00701224 / $16.99
VOL. 118 – ERIC JOHNSON	00701353 / $16.99

VOL. 119 – AC/DC CLASSICS	00701356 / $17.99
VOL. 120 – PROGRESSIVE ROCK	00701457 / $14.99
VOL. 121 – U2	00701508 / $16.99
VOL. 123 – LENNON & MCCARTNEY ACOUSTIC	00701614 / $16.99
VOL. 124 – MODERN WORSHIP	00701629 / $14.99
VOL. 125 – JEFF BECK	00701687 / $16.99
VOL. 126 – BOB MARLEY	00701701 / $16.99
VOL. 127 – 1970S ROCK	00701739 / $14.99
VOL. 128 – 1960S ROCK	00701740 / $14.99
VOL. 129 – MEGADETH	00701741 / $16.99
VOL. 131 – 1990S ROCK	00701743 / $14.99
VOL. 132 – COUNTRY ROCK	00701757 / $15.99
VOL. 133 – TAYLOR SWIFT	00701894 / $16.99
VOL. 134 – AVENGED SEVENFOLD	00701906 / $16.99
VOL. 136 – GUITAR THEMES	00701922 / $14.99
VOL. 137 – IRISH TUNES	00701966 / $15.99
VOL. 138 – BLUEGRASS CLASSICS	00701967 / $14.99
VOL. 139 – GARY MOORE	00702370 / $16.99
VOL. 140 – MORE STEVIE RAY VAUGHAN	00702396 / $17.99
VOL. 141 – ACOUSTIC HITS	00702401 / $16.99
VOL. 142 – KINGS OF LEON	00702418 / $16.99
VOL. 144 – DJANGO REINHARDT	00702531 / $16.99
VOL. 145 – DEF LEPPARD	00702532 / $16.99
VOL. 147 – SIMON & GARFUNKEL	14041591 / $16.99
VOL. 148 – BOB DYLAN	14041592 / $16.99
VOL. 149 – AC/DC HITS	14041593 / $17.99
VOL. 150 – ZAKK WYLDE	02501717 / $16.99
VOL. 153 – RED HOT CHILI PEPPERS	00702990 / $19.99
VOL. 156 – SLAYER	00703770 / $17.99
VOL. 157 – FLEETWOOD MAC	00101382 / $16.99
VOL. 158 – ULTIMATE CHRISTMAS	00101889 / $14.99
VOL. 160 – T-BONE WALKER	00102641 / $16.99
VOL. 161 – THE EAGLES – ACOUSTIC	00102659 / $17.99
VOL. 162 – THE EAGLES HITS	00102667 / $17.99
VOL. 163 – PANTERA	00103036 / $17.99
VOL. 166 – MODERN BLUES	00700764 / $16.99
VOL. 168 – KISS	00113421 / $16.99
VOL. 169 – TAYLOR SWIFT	00115982 / $16.99
VOL. 170 – THREE DAYS GRACE	00117337 / $16.99
VOL. 172 – THE DOOBIE BROTHERS	00119670 / $16.99
VOL. 174 – SCORPIONS	00122119 / $16.99
VOL. 176 – BLUES BREAKERS WITH JOHN MAYALL & ERIC CLAPTON	00122132 / $19.99
VOL. 177 – ALBERT KING	00123271 / $16.99
VOL. 178 – JASON MRAZ	00124165 / $17.99

Complete song lists available online.

Prices, contents, and availability subject to change without notice.

HAL·LEONARD® CORPORATION
7777 W. BLUEMOUND RD. P.O. BOX 13819 MILWAUKEE, WI 53213
www.halleonard.com